SCIENCE BEHIND THE COLORS
CUTTLEFISH

by Alicia Z. Klepeis

pogo

Ideas for Parents and Teachers

Pogo Books let children practice reading informational text while introducing them to nonfiction features such as headings, labels, sidebars, maps, and diagrams, as well as a table of contents, glossary, and index.

Carefully leveled text with a strong photo match offers early fluent readers the support they need to succeed.

Before Reading

- "Walk" through the book and point out the various nonfiction features. Ask the student what purpose each feature serves.
- Look at the glossary together. Read and discuss the words.

Read the Book

- Have the child read the book independently.
- Invite him or her to list questions that arise from reading.

After Reading

- Discuss the child's questions. Talk about how he or she might find answers to those questions.
- Prompt the child to think more. Ask: Did you know about cuttlefish before reading this book? What more would you like to learn about them?

This edition is co-published by agreement between Jump! and World Book, Inc.

Jump!
5357 Penn Avenue South
Minneapolis, MN 55419
www.jumplibrary.com

World Book, Inc.
180 North LaSalle Street, Suite 900
Chicago, IL 60601
www.worldbook.com

Library of Congress Cataloging-in-Publication Data

Names: Klepeis, Alicia, 1971- author.
Title: Cuttlefish / Alicia Z. Klepeis.
Description: Minneapolis: Jump!, Inc., [2022]
Series: Science behind the colors | Includes index.
Audience: Ages 7-10
Identifiers: LCCN 2021030826 (print)
Jump! ISBN 9781636903705 (hardcover)
World Book ISBN 9780716646518 (hardcover)
Subjects: LCSH: Cuttlefish—Juvenile literature.
Camouflage (Biology)—Juvenile literature.
Classification: LCC QL430.3.S47 K54 2022 (print)
DDC 594.58—dc23
LC record available at https://lccn.loc.gov/2021030826

Editor: Eliza Leahy
Designer: Emma Bersie

Photo Credits: Thimas Shing, EyeEm/Alamy, cover; Alberto Carrera/Shutterstock, 1; Rich Carey/Shutterstock, 3, 23; Richard Whitcombe/Shutterstock, 4; MichaelStubblefield/iStock, 5; semet/iStock, 6-7; Jnichanan/Shutterstock, 8-9; Laura Dts/Shutterstock, 10; BIOSPHOTO/Alamy, 11; Ninell_Art/iStock, 12-13; blue-sea.cz/Shutterstock, 14-15; Mayumi.K/Shutterstock, 16; Nature Picture Library/Alamy, 17; Nigel Marsh/iStock, 18-19; Michael Nolan/SuperStock, 20-21.

Printed in the United States of America at Corporate Graphics in North Mankato, Minnesota.

TABLE OF CONTENTS

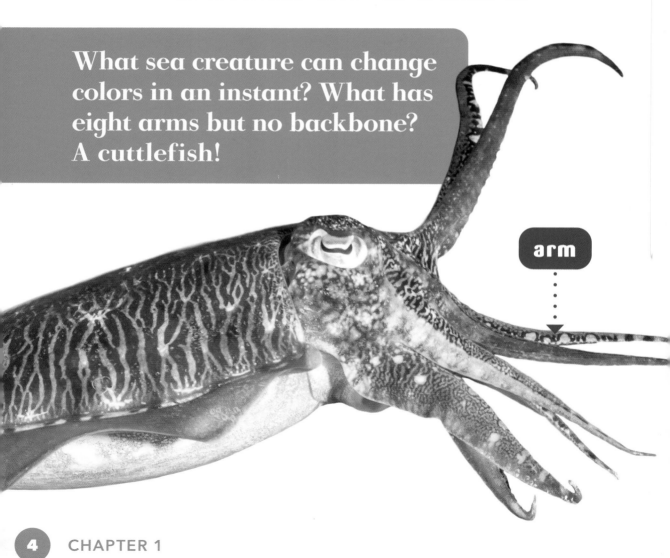

CHAPTER 1

COLORFUL CREATURES

What sea creature can change colors in an instant? What has eight arms but no backbone? A cuttlefish!

arm

There are more than 120 cuttlefish **species**. They live in oceans around the world. Many live in **coral reefs**. The broadclub cuttlefish is one. It changes color to blend in.

broadclub cuttlefish

coral reef

Cuttlefish are **mollusks**, like squid and octopuses. Their bodies are soft.

Some are as small as golf balls. Others are longer than baseball bats!

Cuttlefish use their arms to walk on the ocean floor. They swim by waving their fins up and down. If they need to move quickly, they use their siphons. Siphons shoot water out. This moves cuttlefish backward!

TAKE A LOOK!

What are the parts of a cuttlefish called? Take a look!

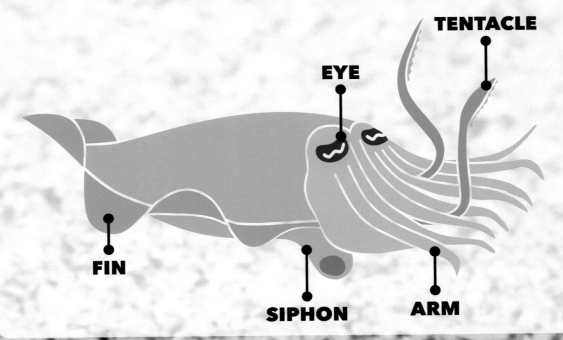

TENTACLE

EYE

FIN

SIPHON

ARM

CHAPTER 2

BLENDING IN

Cuttlefish are **carnivores**. They eat fish, crabs, and shrimp. When a cuttlefish hunts, its color works as **camouflage**. It hides until **prey** gets close. Then it quickly grabs it with its **tentacles**. It pulls the prey into its mouth. *Gulp!*

Sharks and sea lions hunt cuttlefish. Dolphins do, too. But cuttlefish are smart. They can squirt clouds of ink out of their siphons. This hides the cuttlefish. It gives them time to escape.

ink

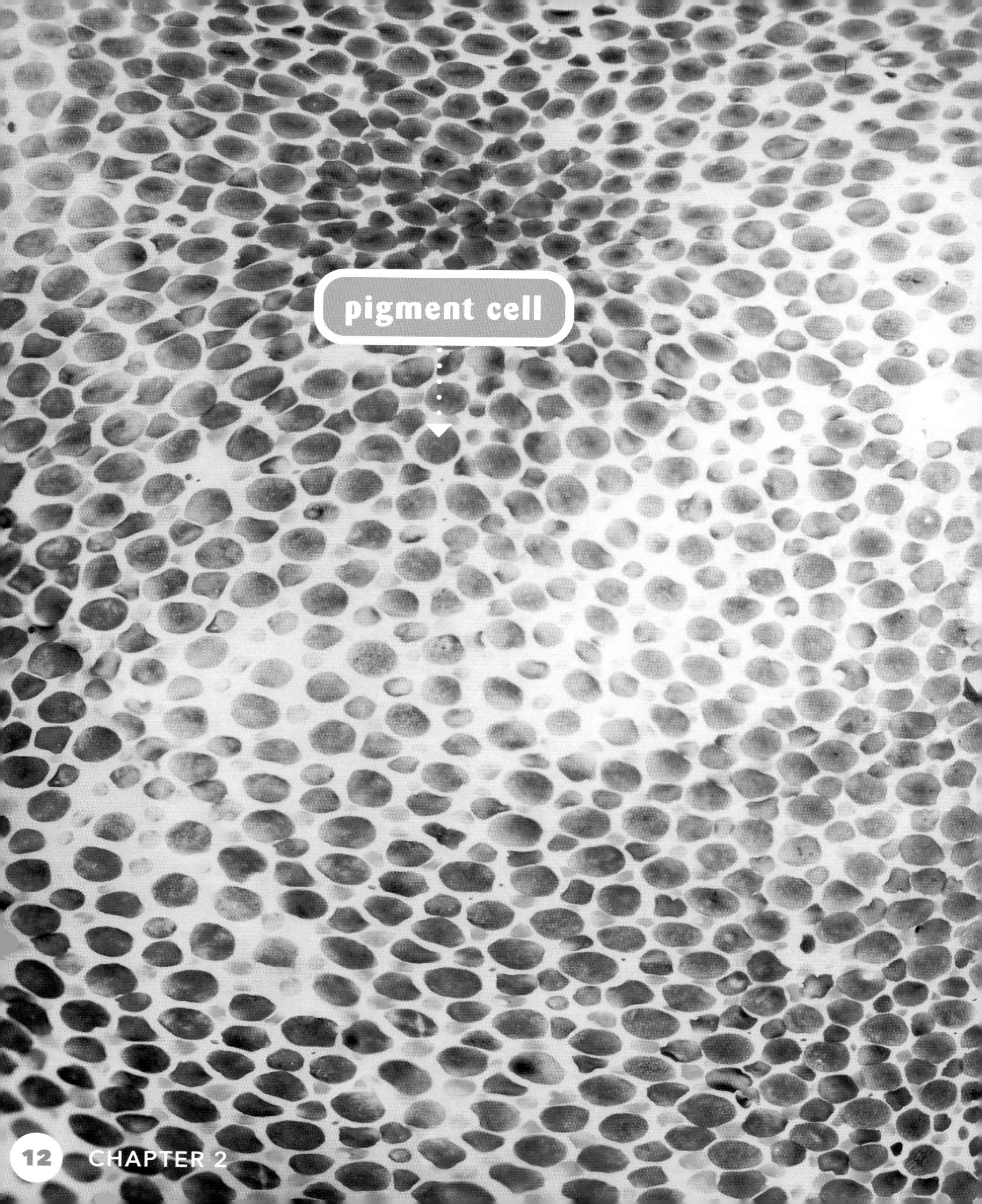
pigment cell

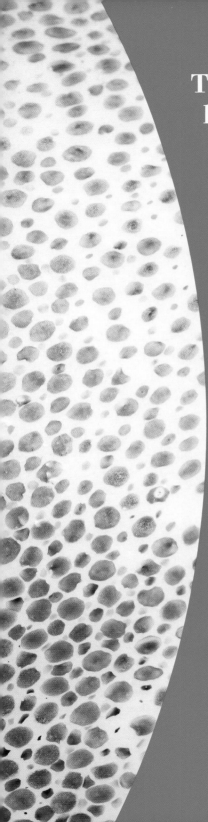

They can also change color to hide from **predators**. Their skin has special **cells** filled with **pigment**. The cells attach to muscles. A cuttlefish's brain tells the muscles what to do.

If they stretch, pigment is released. It goes to the outer layer of the skin. It changes the cuttlefish's color. If they relax, the pigment goes away. The skin underneath shows.

DID YOU KNOW?

Cuttlefish are colorful inside, too. Their blood is bluish green!

They can also change their **patterns** and **textures**! How? Their brains send messages to bumps in their skin. The bumps are like balloons. They get bigger to change size and shape.

DID YOU KNOW?

Cuttlefish are sometimes called chameleons of the sea. Why? They can change color very quickly!

CHAPTER 3

COLOR FOR THE WIN

Cuttlefish also change color to stand out. Bright colors scare predators.

Males flash bold patterns and colors at each other. Why? This is how they fight over females. Their colors warn other males to stay away.

Males also change color to **attract** females. Giant cuttlefish do this. After **mating**, females lay eggs.

DID YOU KNOW?

Cuttlefish change color throughout their lives. They can even change while still in their eggs!

giant
cuttlefish

Cuttlefish use color in many ways. They use it to hunt. They also use it to scare other animals. Would you like to see one of these colorful mollusks?

ACTIVITIES & TOOLS

SEEING THROUGH INK

Cuttlefish squirt ink to hide from predators. See how it works with this activity!

What You Need:
- computer
- printer
- scissors
- clear cup or glass
- tape
- water
- washable brown paint

1. **Print out a picture of a cuttlefish from the internet. Use scissors to cut it out. The picture should fit on one side of the clear cup.**

2. **Tape the picture onto the outside of the cup. Position it so that you can look through the cup and see the cuttlefish.**

3. **Fill the cup with water. How does the cuttlefish look?**

4. **Add two drops of brown paint to the water. Gently swirl it around. Look at the cuttlefish now. Is it more difficult to see? Add two more drops of paint. Does this change how well you see the cuttlefish?**

GLOSSARY

attract: To get something's interest.

camouflage: A disguise or natural coloring that allows animals to hide by making them look like their surroundings.

carnivores: Animals that eat meat.

cells: The smallest units of animals and plants.

coral reefs: Long lines of coral that lie in warm, shallow waters.

mating: Joining together to produce young.

mollusks: Animals with soft bodies and no spines that live in water or damp habitats.

patterns: Repeating arrangements of colors, shapes, or figures.

pigment: A substance that gives color to something.

predators: Animals that hunt other animals for food.

prey: An animal that is hunted by other animals for food.

species: One of the groups into which similar animals and plants are divided.

tentacles: The long, flexible limbs of some ocean animals.

textures: The ways things feel.

INDEX

TO LEARN MORE

Finding more information is as easy as 1, 2, 3.

1 Go to www.factsurfer.com

2 Enter "cuttlefish" into the search box.

3 Choose your book to see a list of websites.

FACT SURFER

[5]